First World War
and Army of Occupation
War Diary
France, Belgium and Germany

5 CAVALRY DIVISION
Divisional Troops
Royal Army Service Corps
Divisional Ammunition Park (72 Company A.S.C.)
1 October 1916 - 16 November 1917

WO95/1163/11

The Naval & Military Press Ltd
www.nmarchive.com
Published in association with The National Archives

Published by

The Naval & Military Press Ltd

Unit 10 Ridgewood Industrial Park,

Uckfield, East Sussex,

TN22 5QE England

Tel: +44 (0) 1825 749494

www.naval-military-press.com

www.nmarchive.com

This diary has been reprinted in facsimile from the original. Any imperfections are inevitably reproduced and the quality may fall short of modern type and cartographic standards.

© **Crown Copyright**
Images reproduced by permission of The National Archives, London, England, 2015.

Contents

Document type	Place/Title	Date From	Date To
Heading	WO95/1163/11		
Heading	5th Cav Div Ammo Park 72 (coy A S C) 1916 Oct-1917 Nov		
Heading	5th Cavalry Div. Amm. Park. 72 Coy A. S. C. Army Service Corps. Nov 1917		
Heading	5th. Cavalry Divisional Ammunition Park 72nd. Coy., A. S. C. Form 19th Sept 1914		
Miscellaneous	5th Cavalry Divisional Ammunition Park 72nd Coy., A. S. C.		
Miscellaneous	Commanding Officers Appendix "A"		
Miscellaneous	Honours And Awards Appendix "B"		
Miscellaneous	5th. Cavalry Divisional Ammunition Park.		
Heading	War Diary of Ammunition Park 5th Cavalry Div (late 2nd. Cavy Divn) From 1st October 1916 To 30th November 1916		
War Diary	Bussy Les Daours	01/10/1916	06/10/1916
War Diary	Montagne	07/10/1916	31/10/1916
Miscellaneous	Appendix A To War Diary for the Month of October 1916		
War Diary	Oust Marest	01/11/1916	10/11/1916
War Diary	Mers	11/11/1916	30/11/1916
Miscellaneous	Appendix "A" To War Diary For the Month of November 1916		
Heading	War Diary of Ammunition Park 5th Cavalry Division From 1st December 1916 To 31st December 1916		
War Diary	Mers	01/12/1916	31/12/1916
Miscellaneous	5th Cavalry Division Ammunition Park Appendix "A" To War Diary for Month of December 1916		
Heading	War Diary of 5th Cavalry Divisional Ammunition Park. From 1st January 1917 To 31st January 1917		
War Diary	Mers	01/01/1917	31/01/1917
Miscellaneous	Appendix "A" To War Diary For The Month January 1917		
Heading	War Diary of 5th Cavalry Div. Am. Park February 1st To 28th 1917 Vol XXVI		
War Diary	Mers	01/02/1917	28/02/1917
Miscellaneous	5th Cavalry Division Ammunition Park Appendix "A" To War Diary For Feby 1917		
Heading	5th Cavalry Div. Amm. Park. March 1st To 31st 1917 Vol XXVII		
War Diary	Marcelcave	01/03/1917	31/03/1917
Miscellaneous	5th Cavalry Division Ammunition Park Appendix "A" To War Diary For The Month of March 1917		
Heading	War Diary of 5th Cavalry Div. Am. Park. April 1st To 30th 1917 Vol XXVIII		
War Diary	Etalon	01/04/1917	30/04/1917
Miscellaneous	5th Cavalry Division Ammunition Park Appendix "A" To War Diary For The Month of April 1917		
Heading	War Diary of 5th Cavalry Div. Am. Park. May 1st To 31st 1917 Vol 29		

War Diary	Tincourt	01/05/1917	31/05/1917
Miscellaneous	5th Cavalry Division Ammunition Park Appendix "A" To War Diary for the Month of May 1917		
Heading	War Diary of 5th Cavalry Divn. Am. Pk June 1st To 30th 1917 Vol XXX		
War Diary	Tincourt	01/06/1917	30/06/1917
Miscellaneous	5th Cavalry Division Ammunition Park Appendix "A" To War Diary For the month of:- June 1917		
Heading	5th Cavalry Divisional Ammunition Park From 1st To 31st July 1917		
War Diary	Tincourt	01/07/1917	16/07/1917
War Diary	St Pol	22/07/1917	29/07/1917
Miscellaneous	5th Cavalry Divisional Ammn. Park. Appendix A to War Diary for the month of July 1917		
Heading	War Diary of 5th Cavalry Divn. Amn. Park. August. Vol XXXII		
War Diary	St Pol	01/08/1917	31/08/1917
Miscellaneous	Appendix A to War Diary of 5th Cavalry Divisional Ammunition Park. for the month of August 1917		
War Diary	War Diary of 5th Cavalry Division Ammn Park September 1917 Vol XXXIII		
War Diary	St Pol	02/09/1917	28/09/1917
Miscellaneous	Appendix A To War Diary of 5th Cavalry Divisional Ammunition Park. For the month of September 1917		
Heading	War Diary of 5th Cavalry Division Ammn Park October 1917 Vol XXXIV		
War Diary	St Pol	02/10/1917	08/10/1917
War Diary	Winnizeele	08/10/1917	18/10/1917
War Diary	Fruges	19/10/1917	31/10/1917
Miscellaneous	Appendix A To War Diary of 5th Cavalry Divisional Ammunition Park. for the mont of October 1917		
War Diary	War Diary of 5th Cavalry Division Amn Park From Nov. 1st-16th November Vol xxxv		
War Diary	Fruges	01/11/1917	16/11/1917
Miscellaneous	5th Cavalry Divisional Ammn Park. Appendix A to War Diary for Period 1st November 17 to 16th November 1917		

WO 95/1163/11

5th CAV DIV Sketch

5th Cav Div Avenue Park
72 (OJ 1150)

1115 OCT — 1417 NOV

From 2 IND CAV DIV
~~No Box~~ Box 1184

To GHQ RES MT COL
Box 134

1163

HISTORICAL RECORD

OF

5th Cavalry Div. Amm. Park.

72 Coy A.S.C.

ARMY SERVICE CORPS.

Recamed 4 GHQ Reser MT Coy
Nov 1917

Appendices

"A" Commanding Officers.
"B" Honours and Awards.
"C" Company Moves.

Notes, or Letters written.

Recorded by:
R. Victor Beveridge
2/Lieut A.S.C.
Oct 1917.

HISTORICAL RECORD

OF

5th. CAVALRY DIVISIONAL AMMUNITION PARK

72nd. COY., A. S. C.

APPENDICES.

"A" — COMMANDING OFFICERS.
"B" — HONOURS AND AWARDS.
"C" — Company Moves.

FORMED 19TH SEPT., 1914.

HISTORICAL RECORD

OF

5th CAVALRY DIVISIONAL AMMUNITION PARK

72nd COY., A.S.C.

1914.

The formation of this Company was completed on the 19th of September, 1914, under command of Capt. H.A.B. CRAWFORD, and consisted of 2 Officers, and 74 O.R. with 14 lorries, 1 Workshop and 1 Store Wagon, with 2 Cars.

The Unit marched from PORTSMOUTH to AVONMOUTH on the 20th. and embarked on the S.Ss. "VETONIA" and "DALCIEST" and on the 23rd. sailed for HAVRE where disembarkation took place on the 25th.

On the 27th. The Unit proceeded by road to ROUEN, via NOMANCOURT, and on the following day marched to VERSAILLES, MONNERVILLE and ORLEANS.

During the month of October the Company was employed in transport work at ORLEANS where the Indian troops were quartered on their arrival in France. The Park moved to CHOCQUES on November 1st. where it was employed in delivering ammunition in small quantities to the Brigade Column.

Up to January 7th. the Unit was designated the Secunderabad Cavalry Brigade Ammunition Park, but on this date the Unit was joined by a new section at AIRE, and thereafter

C.

1914.

was known as the 2nd. Indian Cavalry Divisional Ammunition Park.

This new section was formed at GROVE PARK, and left AVONMOUTH on the 13th. of December, 1914. It consisted of:-

```
Officers  -  2
O.R.      - 80
Lorries   - 20
Cars      -  2
M/cycles  -  3
```

As the Unit was then surplus of lorries, 2 were transferred to 2nd. Indian Cavalry Supply Column and 3 to the 1st Indian Cavalry Ammunition Park: the remainder went to G.H.Q. Troops Supply Column.

1915.

From January 8th to August 1st, 1915, the Park remained at AIRE-SUR-LA-RYS (with the exception of No.2 Section which went to LILLERS and was attached to 1st Corps Ammunition Park from May 3rd to May 25th). It was practically inactive during the whole period, with the exception of the Workshops which were used to repair H.Q. vehicles and in fitting the new lorries with superstructures and accessories.

The Park then moved to various stations, arriving at PONT NOYELLE on August 13th, 1915, where a quantity of Ammunition was delivered; the Park was thus employed until the 15th of September when it moved to FOURDRINOY, and thence to CAMPS-EN-AMIENOIS where six lorries were detached for duty with the AMBALA Cavalry Brigade.

The Headquarters of the Park moved to DOMART on September 22nd.

C.

1 9 1 5.

On October 9th Major H.A.B. CRAWFORD relinquished command of the Park, taking over command of No.2 G.H.Q. Ammunition Park, and was replaced by Capt. W.P.R. WHEATLEY, S. & T.C.

On 21st October the Park, having in the meantime moved to L'ETOILE, was rejoined by the detachment which had been sent to serve the AMBALA Cavalry Brigade, and two days later moved to BIENCOURT.

Capt. H.G.NORMAN WHITE I.A.R. took over command from Capt. WHEATLEY on 21st October, 1915.

At DRUEIL, which was reached on November 17th, all the lorries, with the exception of two British Bernas, were exchanged to make the vehicles homogeneous, the new ones being Swiss Bernas.

1 9 1 6.

On December 17th, the Park was moved to SENARPONT where, on January 22nd, Capt. P.S. WHITCOMBE assumed command. On February 18th, 1916, No.2 Section under Capt. LEE EVANS was attached to 38th Ammunition Sub-Park in the 1st Army for duty, and returned on April 3rd.

On June 4th, 1916, the Park moved to GAMACHES; thence to OISEMONT on the 22nd, and on the 27th eight lorries were sent to G.H.Q. Troops Supply Column on account of the MEERUT Brigade having been withdrawn from the Division thus leaving only the AMBALA and SECUNDERABAD Brigades.

1916.

At BUSSY-LES-DAOURS which was reached on the 27th the Workshop and Store Lorries, together with the Workshop Officer and Artificers, were transferred to G.H.Q. Troops Supply Column owing to the 1st Canadian Cavalry Brigade Ammunition Park being allotted to the Division with its own Workshop and repair staff.

On July 1st, 1916, the remainder of the Park was joined by the Canadian Contingent, the whole being under command of Major MORRISON, Canadian A.S.C.

On July 2nd, Capt. COCKRANE, Canadian R.F.A., took over command from Major MORRISON who was transferred to the 1st Cavalry Sub-Park.

Captain WHITCOMBE was ordered on July 19th., at MERICOURT, to take over command of the combined Sections, and Capt. COCKRANE transferred to the Canadian Corps.

On September 12th the Park, being then at BUSSY-LES-DOURS, commenced to form an Ammunition dump at LA BOISELLE consisting of :-

N.	(13 pr.)	10,000 Rounds.
NX.	(" ")	10,000 "
A.	(18 pr.)	3,600 "
AX.	(" ")	3,600 "
E.		300 "
SAA.		500,000 "

This work was completed on the 14th, and the Park moved that day to ALBERT which was intermittently shelled until the 16th when, in consequence of increasing fire, the lorries were spread out in the fields and along the roads.

1916.

On the night of the 21st September at 9.15 p.m., the dump at LA BOISELLE was hit by a shell and blew up, fortunately without any casualties.

Owing to the continuous shelling of ALBERT it was considered advisable to remove the Park and on the 22nd September it marched to MEAULTE, a few kilometres outside of the town. On the following day it moved back to BUSSY.

On September 26th, the S.A.A. Section proceeded to RAMBURES and went on to MONTAGNE where it billeted.

On October 6th, 1916, the 13 pounder Section, consisting of eight lorries, went to BUIRE for attachment to the 14th Ammunition Sub-Park: the Canadian Section proceeded to MARICOURT to be attached to XIV Corps Ammunition Park: the Headquarters and Workshops marched to MONTAGNE and joined the S.A.A. Section there.

On November 10th, the Headquarters and S.A.A. Sections arrived at MERS-LES-BAINS; the Canadian Section rejoined there on the 12th and on the 19th the 13 pounder Section came in completing the Park.

The title of the Unit was, on November 26th, altered to 5th Cavalry Division Ammunition Park.

1917.

Up to February 11th, 1917, the vehicles of the Park were employed on various fatigues and Engineer Services together with some Ammunition duty.

1917.

On February 12th, the Canadian Section with its vehicles, but without Workshop and Store, together with its Artificer Staff was transferred to the 5th Cavalry Divisional Supply Column and the Park was then brought up to its strength by the arrival of 15 Swiss Berna lorries with drivers, and a British Workshop Staff. The Unit therefore again became an Imperial one.

On March 21st, 1917, the Park moved to QUEVAVILLERS and on the following day went on to MARCELCAVE. On April 15th a move was made to ETALON where a considerable amount of work was done for Engineer Services.

On May 21st, the Park was at TINCOURT where the Corps Park was joined, and every available lorry was employed on Ammunition and Road material in the PERONNE-ROISEL district.

On the night of July 9th, the Unit came under the orders of its Division, ceasing its connection with the Cavalry Corps Park, and on the 16th marched to ST. POL.

A 13 pounder section proceeded with the 17th R.H.A. Brigade to GAUCHIN-LE-GAL, and moved on the 29th to HERSIN, and came under orders of the Canadian Corps Ammunition Park, returning to Headquarters on September 9th.

APPENDIX "A"

COMMANDING OFFICERS
****

September 19th, 1914   -   CAPTAIN H.A.B. CRAWFORD.

October 9th, 1915   -   CAPTAIN W.B.R. WHEATLEY.

October 21st, 1915   -   CAPTAIN H.G. NORMAN WHITE.

January 22nd, 1916   -   CAPTAIN P.S. WHITCOMBE.

July 2nd, 1916   -   CAPTAIN COCKRANE.

July 19th, 1916   -   CAPTAIN P.S. WHITCOMBE.

HONOURS AND AWARDS
****

M.S.M. SPALDING, W.E. - MILITARY CROSS.

APPENDIX "B"

5th. CAVALRY DIVISIONAL AMMUNITION PARK.

PLACE.	FROM.	TO.
PORTSMOUTH.		20th.Sept.1914.
AVONMOUTH.	20th.Sept.1914.	23rd.Sept.1914.
HAVRE.	25th.Sept.1914.	27th.Sept.1914.
ROUEN.	27th.Sept.1914.	28th.Sept.1914.
NONANCOURT.	28th.Sept.1914.	29th.Sept.1914.
VERSAILLES.	29th.Sept.1914.	1st.Oct. 1914.
MONNERVILLE.	1st.Oct. 1914.	2nd.Oct. 1914.
ORLEANS.	2nd.Oct. 1914.	25th.Oct. 1914.
ALLONES.	25th.Oct. 1914.	26th.Oct. 1914.
LOUVIERS.	26th.Oct. 1914.	27th.Oct. 1914.
NEUFCHATEL.	27th.Oct. 1914.	28th.Oct. 1914.
ABBEVILLE.	28th.Oct. 1914.	30th.Oct. 1914.
AIRE.	30th.Oct. 1914.	31st.Oct. 1914.
St.VENANT.	31st.Oct. 1914.	1st.Nov. 1914.
CHOCQUES.	1st.Nov. 1914.	16th.Nov. 1914.
RIEUX.	16th.Nov. 1914.	8th.Jan. 1915.
AIRE.	8th.Jan. 1915.	1st.Aug. 1915.
HUMBERT.	1st.Aug. 1915.	2nd. Aug.1915.
DOMQUERUR.	2nd.Aug. 1915.	3rd.Aug. 1915.
LONGPRE.	3rd.Aug. 1915.	7th.Aug. 1915.
FOURDRINOY.	7th.Aug. 1915.	13th.Aug. 1915.
PONT NOYELLE.	13th.Aug. 1915.	15th.Sept.1915.
FOURDRINOY.	15th.Sept.1915.	17th.Sept.1915.
CAMPS-EN-AMIENOIS.	17th.Sept.1915.	22nd.Sept.1915.
DOMART.	22nd.Sept.1915.	13th.Oct. 1915.
L'TOILE	13th.Oct. 1915.	23rd.Oct. 1915.
BIENCOURT.	23rd.Oct. 1915.	17th.Nov. 1915.

PLACE.	FROM.	TO.
DRUEIL.	17th. Nov. 1915.	17th. Dec. 1915.
SENARPONT.	17th. Dec. 1915.	4th. June 1916.
GAMACHES.	4th. June 1916.	22nd. June 1916.
OISEMONT.	22nd. June 1916.	27th. June 1916.
BUSSY-LES-DAOURS.	27th. June 1916.	17th. July 1916.
MERICOURT.	17th. July 1916.	8th. Aug. 1916.
BOUILLANCOURT.	8th. Aug. 1916.	10th. Aug. 1916.
RAMBURES.	10th. Aug. 1916.	6th. Sept. 1916.
BUSSY-LES-DAOURS.	6th. Sept. 1916.	14th. Sept. 1916.
ALBERT.	14th. Sept. 1916.	22nd. Sept. 1916.
MEAULTE.	22nd. Sept. 1916.	23rd. Sept. 1916.
BUSSY-LES-DAOURS.	23rd. Sept. 1916.	6th. Oct. 1916.
MONTAGNE.	6th. Oct. 1916.	31st. Oct. 1916.
OUST MAREST.	31st. Oct. 1916.	10th. Nov. 1916.
MERS-LES-BAINS.	10th. Nov. 1916.	21st. March 1917.
QUEVAVILLERS.	21st. Mar. 1917.	22nd. Mar. 1917.
MARCELCAVE.	22nd. Mar. 1917.	8th. Apl. 1917.
CHUIGNES.	8th. Apl. 1917.	15th. APL. 1917.
ETALON.	15th. APL. 1917.	13th. May 1917.
POTTE.	13th. May 1917.	21st. May 1917.
TINCOURT.	21st. May 1917.	16th. July 1917.
ST. POL.	16th. July	

5 Cavalry Div. Troops

SERIAL NO. 55

Confidential

Oct 1916 to Nov 1917

War Diary

(72 Cav ASC)

of

Park
Ammunition Column, 5th Cavalry Div. (late 2nd Ind. Cavy. Div).

FROM 1st October 1916 TO 30th November 3rd October 1916.

WAR DIARY or INTELLIGENCE SUMMARY.

Army Form C. 2118.

(Erase heading not required.)

Sheet J

Hour, Date, Place	Summary of Events and Information	Remarks and References to Appendices
BUSSY LES DAOURS. October 1st, 2nd	Nothing to report.	
" 3rd	Grenades No 5 drawn from CONTAY by SAA Section and issued to units	
" 4th	Nothing to report.	
" 5th	Orders rec'd for Canadian 13pr Section to proceed to MARICOURT for attachment to XIV Corps Park. Section left about 12 noon under L' YOUNG. Orders rec'd for Indian 13pr Section to move tomorrow to BUIRE for attachment to XV Corps Park	
" 6th	2' Indian 13pr Section under L' DRURY left at 10am and proceeded via QUERRIEUX, PIREMONT to BUIRE for attachment to No 14 A.S.P. H Q Section of Park left BUSSY at 2.30 pm and moved back to join SAA Section at MONTAGNE, via AMIENS and MOLLIENS VIDAMES arriving at 6 pm.	
MONTAGNE " 7th	SAA issued to Poona Horse	
" 8th, 9th, 10th, 11th	Nothing of importance to report.	
" 12th	SAA issued to Am" Column.	
" 13th, 14th, 15th, 16th	Nothing to report.	
" 17th	SAA issued to Deccan Horse.	
" 18th	ADAS.T Cav Corps arrived with OC ASC about 3.30 pm and inspected Workshop Lorries.	
" 19th	Shooting Competition arranged for men at a Small Machine Gun range in the village.	

WAR DIARY or INTELLIGENCE SUMMARY

Army Form C. 2118.

Hour, Date, Place	Summary of Events and Information	Remarks and References to Appendices
MONTAGNE October 20th	S.A.A. and Grenades Nº 5 issued to Column and today to complete Park drawn from railhead at CONTAY. Running out springs for guns sent up to 13th Section at BUIRE. Shooting Competition took place.	
" 21st, 22nd, 23rd, 24th, 25th–26th	Nothing of importance to report. Weather very bad.	
" 27th	4 sets of running out springs sent up to 13th Section at BUIRE.	
" 28th	Orders recd for G. Lorries to change S.A.A. ammn and proceed to DARGNIES to fetch Armr Plugs at 7 am tomorrow.	
" 29th	G Lorries left for DARGNIES at 7 am for Armr Plugs, returning to Park about 6.30 pm.	
" 30th	Nothing to report.	
" 31st	3 sets of gun springs sent up to 13th Section at BUIRE. Orders recd at 10 am to hand over recce to OUST MAREST, and dump all ammn then 2 Lorries then to be sent back to Subordinated Bde at CROUY and to back to MONTAGNE for night, the latter to report to Anibala Bdr at MOLLIENS VIDAMET next morning. Orders carried out accordingly. Park leaving MONTAGNE at 1.10 pm and moving via OISEMONT and GAMACHES, arriving at MAREST at 5 pm. NOTE. Parades and Lectures were held during the month according to the weather, and all the guns were put through a shooting course. The weather during the latter part of the month was very bad.	P.S. Whitcombe Capt RFA Commdg 2nd Indian Div Ammn Park 1/11/16

(9 29 6) W 3332—1107 100,000 10/13 H W V Forms/C. 2118/10.

Appendix "A".

War Diary for the month of October 1916.

Date.	To whom issued.	Nature of Ammn.	Number Issued.	Remarks.
3.10.16	3 Brigades, 2 S.C.D.	Grenades Hand No 5.	300.	
6.10.16	— do —	— do —	450.	
7.10.16	Poona Horse.	S.A.A. "303".	5,000.	
12.10.16	Amn Col. 2 S.C.D.	S.A.A. "303".	30,000.	
16.10.16	Divl Headquarters	Pistol Webley	276.	
17.10.16	Deccan Horse	S.A.A. "303"	4,000.	
" "	"	Pistol Webley	276.	
20.10.16	Amn Col; 2 S.C.D.	S.A.A "303"	35,000.	
" "	"	Pistol Webley	4140.	
" "	"	Grenades No.5.	168.	

P.S.Vincent Captain a.a.c.
Cmdg, 2 S.Ld; Sdn; Amn; Park.

WAR DIARY or INTELLIGENCE SUMMARY.

(Erase heading not required.)

Army Form C. 2118.

Sheet I

Hour, Date, Place	Summary of Events and Information	Remarks and references to Appendices
OUST MAREST November 1st	The 10 lorries from Ambala Bde. returned to the Park about 6.30 pm, and the 2 lorries from Secunderabad Bde. at 8.30 pm. Orders received for 10 lorries to be at Ordnance Dump at SENARPONT at 10 am tomorrow.	
" 2nd	12 lorries out on Ordnance fatigue, 10 at SENARPONT and 2 at SOUES.	
" 3rd	Nothing to report.	
" 4th	10 lorries on fatigue at BLANGY for conveying hay to Cav. Cav. Regts.	
" 5th, 6th, 7th	Nothing to report.	
" 8th	SAA issued to Secunderabad Machine Gun Squadron.	
" 9th	Information received that Park would probably move to MERS tomorrow. 4 lorries returned to Park from 13th Section with cracked chassis.	
" 10th	Park left OUST MAREST at 2 pm and moved to MERS, arriving at 2.30 pm.	
MERS " 11th	Nothing to report.	
" 12th	SAA issued to Divisional School. Canadian 13th Section returned to Park from 14th Corps Park, arriving at 6.30 pm.	
" 13th	Grenades No 5 issued to Divl School. 2 of the lorries with cracked chassis evacuated to railhead, and replacements demanded.	
" 14th	Nothing to report.	
" 15th	4 lorries sent up to 13th Section, attached to No 14 A.S.P. to enable it to return complete with ammunition. Remaining 2 lorries with cracked chassis evacuated to railhead.	
" 16th	Census Inspector from DAT came to inspect the Vehicle Register.	

WAR DIARY or INTELLIGENCE SUMMARY.

Army Form C. 2118.

(Erase heading not required.)

Sheet II

Hour, Date, Place	Summary of Events and Information	Remarks and references to Appendices
MERS November 17	4 lorries required for R.E work left to be attached to Div" Supply Column at WOINCOURT. Probable duration of duty about 1 week.	
" 18	Nothing to report.	
" 19	13 L Section under Lt DRURY returned to Park from No 14 A.S.P., Complete with Ammunition, and having another lorry with a cracked chassis.	
" 20	Nothing to report.	
" 21	S.A.A. and 3 pr am" issued to LAC Battery	
" 22	Nothing to report.	
" 23	Ammunition drawn from Supply railhead WOINCOURT.	Appendix "A"
" 24	Ammunition drawn from railhead yesterday issued.	" "A"
" 25	Nothing to report.	
" 26	Title of Park changed from 2nd Indian to 5th Cavalry Div" Am" Park.	
" 27, 28, 29	Nothing to report.	
" 30	S.A.A. and 1" Very Lights issued to Secunderabad M.G. Squadron, and 1" Very Lights issued to 9th Hodson's Horse. NOTE. The weather during the month has been very variable with a fair amount of rain, but the roads in the present area have not been bad.	

J.S. Wisemen Capt ASC
Comdg 5th Cavalry Div" Am" Park

1/12/16.

Appendix "E" to War Diary for the month of November 1916.

Date	To whom issued	Nature of Ammn.	Number of Rounds	Remarks
Nov. 5th	Secunderabad M.G. Squad	S.A.A.	45,000	
" 12th	Divisional School	"	2,000	
" 19th	" "	Rounds No 5.	960.	
" 19th	" "	S.A.A.	1,000	
" 21st	No 9 Light Armoured Car Battery	S.A.A.	3,000.	
" "	" " "	"E"	205.	
" 24th	Anti-gas school	P. Smoke	50.	
" "	Divisional school	Smoke candle	50.	
" "	" "	Rounds Mk9	960.	
" "	" "	No 23	560.	
" "	" "	No 20	160.	
" 30th	Secunderabad M.G. Squadron	P. Smoke	46.	
" "	" " "	S.A.A.	6,000.	
" "	" " "	1" Very Light	12 doz.	
" "	9th Hodson Horse	1" "	60 boxes	

72 M.T.Co. A.S.C.
1 DEC 1916
CAV. AMMN. PARK

P.S.Mint, Captain A.S.C.
Comdg 2nd Cavalry Div.
Ammn. Park.

SERIAL NO. 55

Confidential
War Diary

of

Ammunition Park, 5th Cavalry Division

FROM 1st December 1916 TO 31st December 1916.

WAR DIARY or INTELLIGENCE SUMMARY.

Army Form C. 2118.

Hour, Date, Place	Summary of Events and Information	Remarks and references to Appendices
MERS.		
December 1st to 7th	Nothing of importance to report. Weather fair.	
" 8th	12 pr and SAA issued to Ammunition Column.	
" 9th	SAA issued to Light Armoured Car Battery.	
" 10th, 11th	Nothing to report.	
" 12th	G.O.C Division inspected the tickets of the unit at 11.45 am.	
" 13th	Nothing to report.	
" 14th	An Officer of Inspection Branch came to see the Swiss Brown lorry with cracked chassis	
" 15th	SAA issued to Ambulance Bde.	
" 16th	Nothing to report.	
" 17th	SAA issued to Divisional School. Lorry with cracked chassis evacuated to Paris	
" 18th, 19th, 20th	Nothing to report.	
" 21st	G.O.C. Division inspected the Park at 2.30 pm.	
" 22nd	SAA issued to 9th L.A.C. Battery. Alteria lorry arrived from Park Depôt Troupes S.C. to replace Swiss Brown evacuated to Bassens Heavy Repair Shops	
" 23rd	SAA issued to Amn Column.	
" 24th	Grenades No 5 issued to Ambulance Bde.	
" 25th	12 lorries sent to lift the Supply Column delivering rations.	

WAR DIARY
or
INTELLIGENCE SUMMARY.
(Erase heading not required.)

Army Form C. 2118.

Sheet II.

Hour, Date, Place	Summary of Events and Information	Remarks and references to Appendices
MERS		
December 26th	Nothing to report.	
" 27th	Lt. DRURY went to interview A.Q.M.G. Cavalry Corps with reference to his application for a Regular Commission.	
" 28th	Nothing to report.	
" 29th	S.A.A. issued to 9th Hodson's Horse.	
" 30th	8 lorries out under Lt. DRURY conveying troops to ABBEVILLE.	
" 31st	S.A.A. issued to Canadian Amm Column.	
	NOTE. With the exception of two roads during the month, the roads were generally wet but otherwise good. Opportunity has been taken to clean overhaul all lorries requiring it, and good progress has been made.	
1/1/17		P.S. Whincup Capt RFC Cmdg 5th Cavalry Amm Park

5th Cavalry Divisional Ammunition Park

Appendix "A" to War Diary for month of December.

Date	To whom issued.	Nature of ammunition issued.	Number of Rounds.	Remarks
Dec. 8th	Ammunition Column, 5th Cavalry Div.	N.	268.	
" 8th	" " " "	N.X.	140.	
" 8th	" " " "	S.H.A.	4,000.	
" 8th	No. 9. Light Armoured Car Battery.	"	3,000.	
" 13th	Ambala Cavalry Brigade.	"	12,000.	
" 19th	Divisional school, 5th Cav. Div.	"	5,000.	
" 22nd	No. 9. Light Armoured Car Battery.	"	1,000.	
" 23rd	Ammunition Column, 5th Cavalry Div.	Lewis Land Vrs	480.	
" 24th	Ambala Brigade.	S.H.A.	24,000.	
" 29th	9th Hodson's Horse.	"	26,000.	
" 31st	Canadian Amn: Column.	Rifle Volley.	2,760.	

P.S. Winch Captain. A.S.C.
O/C 5th Cavalry Div.
Amn: Park.

SERIAL NO. 55

Confidential
War Diary
of

72 Coy ASC

5th CAVALRY DIVISIONAL AMMUNITION PARK.

FROM 1st January 1917 1911 TO 31st January 1917 191

WAR DIARY
or
INTELLIGENCE SUMMARY.
(Erase heading not required.)

Army Form C. 2118.

Sheet I

Hour, Date, Place	Summary of Events and Information	Remarks and references to Appendices
MERS. January 1st & 2nd	Nothing to Report.	
" 3rd	22 lorries conveyed Section Pioneer Battn from GAMACHES to billets.	
" 4th	Nothing to report.	
" 5th	Capt. Whitcombe attended lecture on Ammn Supply at HESDIN	
" 6th	Explosives collected from Supply Railhead WOINCOURT.	
" 7th	3 lorries sent to Divl Purchasing Officer for duty.	
" 8th	Nothing to report	
" 9th	S.A.A. issued to XX Horse, Poona Horse, & Ambala. M.G.S.	
" 10th, 11th & 12th	Nothing to report.	
" 13th	Pistol Webley to Fort Garry Horse.	
" 14th & 15th	Nothing to report. Ammn issued to M.G.S. Canadian Bde	
" 16th	Grenades to Sec'bad Brigade, Ambala Brigade & Canadian Bde.	
" 17th	S.A.A. issued to 9th Light Armoured Car Battery & Pistol Webley Ammunition issued to 34th Poona Horse.	
" 18th	Webley Pistol, & S.A.A. issued to Ammunition Column	
" 19th, 20th & 21st	Nothing to report	
" 22nd	Pistol Webley & S.A.A. issued to 8th Hussars. 3 lorries went to ROUEN, to fetch petrol for French Customs	
" 23rd	Nothing to report.	
" 24th	S.A.A. issued to 9th Hodson's Horse	
" 25th	S.A.A. issued to Poona Horse	

WAR DIARY or INTELLIGENCE SUMMARY

Army Form C. 2118.

Sheet II

Hour, Date, Place	Summary of Events and Information	Remarks and references to Appendices
MERS. January 26th	Colt Automatic Ammunition issued to Fort Garry Horse. Capt. Whitcombe went to Divisional Head Quarters on duty for one month.	
" 27th	Nothing to report.	
" 28th	Cavalry Explosives collected from Divisional School.	
" 29th	.303 Ammunition issued to Fort Garry Horse	
" 30th	Nothing to report	
" 31st	Nothing to report.	

Note: The weather throughout the month has cold but fine & the roads in this area have been in good condition.

J.C. Denny Lieut. A.S.C.
for O.C. 5th Cavalry Amm'n Park

Appendix "A" to War Diary
for the month of January 1917.

Date.	To whom issued.	Number Pounds.	Nature Ammn.	Remarks.
9-1-17	M.G.S. Australian Brigade	18,000	S.A.A.	
" "	34th Poona Horse	5,000	"	
" "	20th Deccan Horse	30,000	"	
13.1.17	Lord Strathcona Horse	552	Pistol Webley	
14.1.17	M.G.S. Canadian Brigade	828.	"	
16.1.17	S'bad Brigade	804	Grenade Hand No. 5.	
" "	Ambala Brigade	792	"	
" "	Canadian Brigade	792		
17.1.17	No. 9 L.A.C. Battery	2,000	S.A.A.	
" "	34th Poona Horse	828.	Pistol Webley	
18.1.17	Ammn. Col. 5th C. Div	2252.	"	
" "	"	30,000	S.A.A.	
22.1.17	5th Kurrani	41,000	S.A.A.	
" "	"	828.	Pistol Webley	
24.1.17	9th Hodsons Horse	11,000	S.A.A.	
25.1.17	Poona Horse	33,000	S.A.A.	
26.1.17	"	200.	Colt Automatic	
30.1.17	Lord Strathcona Horse	3,000	S.A.A.	

[signature]
for O.C. 5th C.D.A.P.

CONFIDENTIAL

WAR DIARY

of

5th CAVALRY DIV'N AM'N PARK

February 1st to 28th 1917.

Vol. XXVI

Serial No. 55

WAR DIARY
or
INTELLIGENCE SUMMARY.
(Erase heading not required.)

Army Form C. 2118.

Sheet 1.

Instructions regarding War Diaries and Intelligence Summaries are contained in F. S. Regs., Part II. and the Staff Manual respectively. Title pages will be prepared in manuscript.

Place	Date	Hour	Summary of Events and Information	Remarks and references to Appendices
MERS	February			
-	1st		Nothing to report - Weather very cold & snow.	
-	2nd		Nothing to report.	
-	3rd		18.000 S.A.A. issued to R. Canadian Dragoons - 3 lorries on fatigue duties at AMBREVILLE.	
-	4th		5 lorries detached for duty at Cavalry Corps Headquarters.	
-	5th		Grenades No. 5. issued - 396 to 7th Dragoon Guards. 396 to Poona Horse & 396 to Deccan Horse.	
-	6th		12 lorries on Wood carrying fatigues & lorries carrying Rations for party proceeding to PICQUIGNY	
-	7th		7 lorries on Wood carrying fatigues & 2/Lt. P.H.D. Helm Workshop Officer joined the unit for duty.	
-	8th		10 lorries conveying Pioneer Battn. Secunderabad Bde. to AUTHUILE & conveying Canadian Battn. back to Billets.	
-	9th		Nothing to report.	
-	10th		12 lorries finishing move of Pioneer Battn. to AUTHUILE.	
-	11th		180 rds. Colt Ammn. to Lord Strathcona's Horse.	
-	12th		1176 Grenades No. 5. issued to Sec'bad. Bde - 624 Grenades No. 5. issued to Ambala Brigade. Personnel of Canadian Section transferred to 5th Cavalry Division Supply Column & the necessary British personnel received from them to complete the establishment of Park.	

WAR DIARY
or
INTELLIGENCE SUMMARY.
(Erase heading not required.)

Army Form C. 2118.

Sheet II

Place	Date	Hour	Summary of Events and Information	Remarks and references to Appendices
MERS	February 13th		Nothing of importance to Report.	
"	14th		Nothing to report.	
"	15th		17 Lorries on duty drawing Ammunition from Railhead.	
"	16th		13 prs & S.A.A. issued to Canadian Amm'n Column. 3 prs issued to L.A. Car Batty. No. 5 Grenades issued to Amm'n Column, 18th Lancers & Machine Gun Sqd. Rimbala Bde.	
"	17th		4 lorries conveying Stores to ABANCOURT. 1 Pistol Illuminating issued to M.G. Sqd.	
"	18th		Nothing to report.	
"	19th		Nothing to report.	
"	20th		Pistols Webley Amm'n issued to XX Deccan Horse. Thaw scheme in operation.	
"	21st		Pistols Webley Amm'n issued to Royal Canadian Dragoons.	
"	22nd		Nothing to report.	
"	23rd		10 Men on road fatigues daily at DARGNIES.	
"	24th		Nothing to report.	
"	25th		S.A.A. issued to 18th Lancers Swiss Berna lorry evacuated to Base with cracked chassis	
"	26th		S.A.A. issued to Canadian Bde Machine Gun Sqd.	
"	27th		5 lorries on duty with S.O.D.T. at ABBEVILLE. Pistol Webley Amm to 7.9 Horse T	
"	28th		S.A.A. issued to Light A. Car Batty.	S.A.A to L.S Horse

J Drury Lieut. A.S.C.
For O/C 5th Cavalry Amm'n Park

5th Cavalry Divisional Ammn: Park.

Appendix "A" to War Diary for Feby 1917.

Date	To whom issued	Number rounds	Nature of ammn.	Remarks
3.2.17	Royal Canadian Dragoons	18,000	S.A.A. ".303"	
5.2.17	7th Dragoon Guards	396	Grenade No. 5.	
"	34th Poona Horse	396	"	
"	20th Deccan Horse	396	"	
11.2.17	Lord Strathcona Horse	180	L.H. Automatic	
12.2.17	S. Ld. Brigade	1176	Grenade No. 5.	
"	Ambala Brigade	624	"	
16.2.17	Canadian Amm. Col.	1302	Aeroplane	
"	"	231	N.E. } 13pdr.	
"	"	24,000	S.A.A. "303"	
"	L.A.C. Battery	32	3 Pdr.	
"	"	1536	Grenade No. 5.	
"	5 Cavy Div. Amm Col.	6	"	
"	18th Lancers	78	"	
"	K. Ed. Ambala Bde.	2532	Pistol Verey	
20.2.17	20th Deccan Horse	828	"	
21.2.17	Royal Canadian Dragoons	15,000	S.A.A. "303"	
25.2.17	18th Lancers	20,000	"	
26.2.17	K. Ed. Own Cav. Bde.	1152	Pistol Verey	
27.2.17	Fort Garry Horse	6,000	S.A.A. "303"	
"	"	24,000	"	
28.2.17	Lord Strathcona Horse	13,000	S.A.A. "303"	
"	L.A.C. Battery			

Murry
for O.C. 5th C.D.A.P.
Lieut. Act.
O.C. 5th C.D.A.P.

CONFIDENTIAL

WAR DIARY
of
5th CAVALRY DIVn. AMMn. PARK.

MARCH 1st to 31st 1917

Vol XXVII

Serial No. 55.

WAR DIARY or INTELLIGENCE SUMMARY.

Army Form C. 2118.

Sheet. I

Place	Date	Hour	Summary of Events and Information	Remarks and references to Appendices
MARCELCAVE	MARCH 1st		Nothing to report, weather fine.	
-	2nd		S.A.A. issued to Light Armoured Car Battery.	
-	3rd		Lorry conveying party for Road Repairs.	
-	4th		Lorry conveying party to BOULOGNE for Carrier pigeon course.	
-	5th		2 lorries conveying working party to DARGNIES.	
-	6th		Nothing to report.	
-	7+8th		Nothing to report.	
-	9th		2 lorries conveying working party to DARGNIES.	
-	10th		Grenades No 5 collected from 7th Dragoon Guards & Poona Horse. Lorry conveying party to BOULOGNE.	
-	11th		4 lorries drawing Ammn. from R.H.Q.	
-	12th		S.A.A Pistol Webley, No 5 Grenades & 3 pr Ammn. drawn from R.H. to army Col.	
-	13th		S.A.A. to Fort Garry Horse. N & N.X. to Ammn. Col. S.A.A. to Ammn. Col & 3 pr Ammn. to L.A.C.B. 4 lorries issuing Ammn. & 4 lorries on road fatigues DARGNIES.	Col
-	14th		S.A.A to Fort Garry Horse & No. 14. M.G.S. Hotchkiss 9 an praches — S.A.A & P.W. to Ammn. 2 lorries evacuating unserviceable Ammn. at BOULOGNE	Col
-	15th		S.A.A. to R Can Dragoons, Pistol Webley to Fort Garry Horse.	

WAR DIARY or INTELLIGENCE SUMMARY.

Army Form C. 2118.

Sheet II

Place	Date	Hour	Summary of Events and Information	Remarks and references to Appendices
MARCELCAVE	MARCH 16th		4 lorries on Road Fatigues, lorry conveying party to BOLOGNE.	
	17th		S.A.A. issued to R¹ Can. Dragoons - unserviceable N.X. exchanged at BOLOGNE. 4 lorries conveying stores from ABBEVILLE, 2 lorries issuing Amm¹⁸	
	18th		4 lorries on Road fatigues.	
	19th		17 lorries on duty at Divisional Dumps.	
	20th		25 lorries on Duty at Divisional Dumps.	
	21st		Park moved from MERS - to QUEVAVILLERS.	
	22nd		Park moved from QUEVAVILLERS - to MARCELCAVE. - 21 lorries delivering Iron Rations to Brigades - Surplus Grenades collected from Brigades & evacuated. Red Flares drawn from R¹H⁹ & issued to Brigades.	
	23rd		4 lorries on duty with Supply Col. Supply Officer.	
	24th & 25th		Nothing to report.	
	26th		S.A.A. issued to Sec Bad Bde & drawn from R¹H⁹ to complete Est.	
	27th		Unserviceable "N" to O.B R¹H⁹. - S.A.A. issued to Canadian Bde & Amm¹⁸ Col. "N" N.X. S.A.A. & Grenades No.5. issued to R.C.H.A. Amm¹⁸ Col. - Surplus Cavalry explosives collected from Amm¹⁸ Col & evacuated - Amm¹⁸ drawn to complete Est. from R¹H⁹. 4 lorries on Duty.	

WAR DIARY or INTELLIGENCE SUMMARY.

Army Form C. 2118.

Sheet III

Place	Date	Hour	Summary of Events and Information	Remarks and references to Appendices
MARCELCAVE	MARCH 28th		"N" "NX" "S.A.A." & Grenades to 5th R.C.H.A. Ammn Col.	
	29th		4 lorries on duty drawing Ammn from R⁴ʰ	
	30th		"N" & "NX" issued to Ammn Col. & R.C.H.A. Ammn Column.	
			6 lorries conveying parties to R⁴ʰ for Divisional Remounts.	
	31st		S.A.A. to Sec Bak & Canadian Cavalry Brigades —	
			8 lorries drawing fuel for Division, 2 lorries detached with D.A.D.O.S.	

1/4/17.

J. Denny Lieut. A.S.C.
for. O/C 5th Cav. Ammn Park.

5th Cavalry Divisional Ammunition Park.

Appendix "16" to War Diary

for the month of March 1917.

Date	To whom issued	Number of Rounds	Nature of Ammunition	Remarks
2-3-17	L.A.C. Battery	14,000	S.A.A.	
17-2-17	Canadian Cavalry Brigade	708	Grenades No.5	*entries in Feb. Diary
13-3-17	Fort Garry Horse	10,000	S.A.A.	
13-3-17	Amm¹ Col. 5th Cav. Division	12,000	S.A.A.	
" "	" "	990	Shrapnel	
" "	" "	330	H.E.	
" "	" "	100	3 Pdr.	
14-3-17	L.A.C. Battery	10,500	S.A.A.	
" "	No. 14 M.G.S.	12,000	"	
" "	Amm¹ Col. 5th Cav. Division	4,000	"	
" "	" "	1656	Pistol Webley	
15-3-17	R.C.D's	30,000	S.A.A.	
" "	Fort Garry Horse	1932	Pistol Webley	
17-3-17	R.C.D's	20,000	S.A.A.	
26-3-17	Shod Rate 4th Q.M.	12,000	S.A.A.	
27-3-17	Canadian Bde	9,000	S.A.A.	
" "	Amm¹ Col. 5th Cav. Division	3,000	S.A.A.	
28-3-17	R.C.H.A. Amm¹ Col.	152	H.E.	
" "	" "	456	Shrapnel	
" "	" "	33,000	S.A.A.	
30-3-17	Amm¹ Col. 5th Cav. Division	36	Grenade No. 5.	
" "	" "	268	Shrapnel	
" "	" "	40	H.E.	
" "	R.C.H.A. Amm¹ Col.	444	Shrapnel	
" "	" "	34	H.E.	

Lieut. & O.C.
O.C. 5th C.D.A.P.

CONFIDENTIAL. Vol 28

WAR DIARY
of
8th CAVALRY DIV AMM PARK.

April 1st to 30th 1917

Vol XXVIII

Bound No. 55.

WAR DIARY
or
INTELLIGENCE SUMMARY.

Army Form C. 2118.

(Erase heading not required.) I

Place	Date	Hour	Summary of Events and Information	Remarks and references to Appendices
ETALON	1917 April 1st		13p¹ Ammn issued to Ammn Col, 5 lorries on duty. Weather very wet.	
	2nd		24 lorries on Stone fatigues - heavy fall of snow.	
	3rd		13p¹ Ammn issued to Light Section Canadian Ammn Col. and to Light Section Ambala Brigade. 24 lorries on duty - Stone fatigues & delivering Ammn. Ammn drawn from Railhead to complete Establishment.	
	4th		S.A.A. issued to Main Section Canadian Ammn Col. 24 lorries on Road mending fatigues.	
	5th		24 lorries on Road mending fatigues.	
	6th		24 lorries conveying troops & on road fatigues.	
	7th		S.A.A. issued to 8th Hussars, 9th Hussars, & 18 Lancers. Unserviceable 13p¹ Ammn collected from X Battery R.H.A. & returned to Railhead. 24 lorries conveying Ammn from R.H. to New S.A. type dumps TINCOURT.	
	8th		P.W. & S.A.A. issued to Ammn Col Ambala. 3 lb unserviceable 13p¹ exchanged for X Batty R.H.A. S.A.A.(A.P.) drawn from Railhead. The Park moved to road running through R.36 sheet 100.00.	

WAR DIARY or INTELLIGENCE SUMMARY.

Army Form C. 2118.

Place	Date	Hour	Summary of Events and Information	Remarks and references to Appendices
ETALON	1916 Oct 9th		P.W. Amm¹ to Sec¹ bad Bde. S.A.A. (A.P.) issued to Secunderabad, Canadian, Ambala Brigades, & to No. 9 Light Armoured Car Batty. 23 lorries on duty conveying Refugees, & Divisional Dismounted troops, kits to back area.	
	10th		16 lorries on duty conveying tents & fuel to new Divisional Area – 1 lorry taking wheels to Type Press.	
	11th		12 lorries on fuel fatigues for Division. 9 lorries conveying balance of 13th at O.H. & 6 J. Railheads to O.B. R⁴ H⁴.	
	12th		S.A.A. & P.W. Amm¹ to Light Amm¹ Col. Ambala Bde. P.W. Amm¹ to H.Q¹ Ambala Bde. P.W. Amm¹ to Hodson's Horse. S.A.A. to Light Col. Sec¹bad Bde. All supplys completed to date from Railhead. 6 Lorries conveying Div. working party to New Area.	
	13th		S.A.A. (A.P.) issued to each Bde. 20 lorries under Lieut. Chatterton conveying No. 1 London Casualty Clearing Station from GROVETOWN to LA CHAPELETTE. 1 lorry Amm¹ duty.	
	14th		Great Stores drawn & issued to Regt. 18 lorries on Divisional fatigues. 1 lorry & 20 men to Div. H.Q¹ for fatigues.	

WAR DIARY or INTELLIGENCE SUMMARY

Army Form C. 2118.

Place	Date	Hour	Summary of Events and Information	Remarks and references to Appendices
ETALON	1917 April 15th		Green Flares drawn from OJ R.H. & held in reserve. 6 lorries to MERICOURT for Divisional Stores. The Park moved from ROB to ETALON. A.F.B. printed Sheet 66 D.	
	16th		1000 rds 13 pr drawn from R.H. & held in reserve.	
	17th		20 lorries conveying supplies from PROYART to New Div. Area. 1 lorry to Tyl press.	
	18th		15 lorries on Supply & R.E. fatigues NTENCOURT.	
	19th		S.A.A. to L.S.H. & Ammn. Col. 60 Grenades No 5 exchanged Main Sec. Ammn. Col.	
	20th		S.A.A. rec'd Can. Main Col. issued to 5th Div. Amm. Col. 10 lorries conveying huts from CAIX to Div Area. 4 lorries on Supply fatigues.	
	21st		10 lorries conveying huts CAIX to New Div. Area. 10 lorries on R.E. fatigues TERTRY.	
	22nd		4 lorries on duty.	
	23rd		10 lorries conveying huts from CAIX to 35th Div. H.Q. 5 lorries conveying ammn to OJ R.H.	
	24th		1000 rds 13 pr returned to OJ R.H. supplies to Col. S.A.A. & L.S.H. for printed indents. 10 lorries conveying huts CAIX to Div Area. 5 lorries conveying ammn from OJ R.H.	
	25th		10 lorries conveying huts from CAIX to Div Area. 5 lorries on duty OJ R.H. 2 lorries Supply fatigues	
	26th		R.W. Ammn to R.H.A. Bde. 10 lorries conveying huts CAIX to Div Area.	
	27th		S.A.A.(A.P.) drawn from OJ R.H. & issued to Brigades & L.A.C. Batty. 10 lorries conveying huts from CAIX.	

Place	Date	Hour	Summary of Events and Information	Remarks and references to Appendices
ETALON	Apl 1917 28th		S.A.A. issued to 7th Dragoon Guards. 8 lorries conveying huts from CAIX. 2 lorries detached with Field Sqn. R.E. TERTRY.	
	29th		8 lorries conveying huts from CAIX.	
	30th		S.A.A. issued to 8th Hussars & 20th Deccan Horse. 8 lorries conveying huts from CAIX.	

1/5/17

J. Dunn Lieut & Adj
for O/C 5th Cav. Div. Ammn. Park

5th Cavalry Divisional Ammunition Park.

Appendix "A" to War Diary for the month of April 1917.

Date.	To whom issued.	Number of Rounds.	Nature of Ammn.	Remarks.
1-4-17	Ammn Col; 5th Cavy Div;	350.	Shrapnel.	
" "	" " "	88.	H. E.	
3-4-17	Light Arm: Ammn Col; Cavy Bde	204.	Shrapnel.	
" "	" " "	104.	H. E.	
" "	" Ambl: Bde.	8.	H. E.	
4-4-17	Main Sect; Canadian Ammn Col;	28,000.	S. A. A.	
7-4-17	8th Hussars.	12,000.	S. A. A	
" "	9th Hodson's Horse	12,000.	S. A. A.	
" "	18th Lancers.	12,000.	S. A. A.	
8-4-17	Ammn Col. Ambl: Bde.	37,000	S. A. A.	
" "	" "	828	Pistol Webley	
9-4-17	Sialkot Brigade	3312.	S.A.A.(A.P.)	
" "	"	600.	" "	
" "	Canadian Bde.	600.	"	
" "	Ambl: Bde.	600.		
" "	No. 9. L.A.C. Battery;	200.	S. A. A.	
12-4-17	Light Ammt Col: Ambl: Bde.	17,000	S. A. A.	
" "	" " "	276.	Pistol Webley	
" "	Headquarters Ambl: Bde.	100.	"	
13-4-17	9th Hodson's Horse	2760.	S. A. A.	
" "	Light Ammt Col; Sia'kot Bde.	7000	S.A.A(A.P.)	
" "	Sia'kot Bde.	77	S. A. A.	
" "	Canadian Bde.	77	"	
" "	Ambl: Bde.	76	"	
19-4-17	Lord Strathcona Horse;	2400	S. A. A.	
" "	Ammt Col; 5th Cavy Div;	6,000	S. A. A.	
" "	"	828	Pistol Webley	
24-4-17	Lord Strathcona Horse,	2,000	S. A. A.	

P.T.O.

Date:	To whom issued.	Number of rounds.	Nature of ammunition.	Remarks.
26-4-17	17th R.H.A. Bde.	276.	Rifle? bulley?	
27-4-17	Ambala Bde.	240.	S.A.A (A.P)	
" "	Sialkot Bde.	240.	" " "	
" "	Lucknow Bde.	240.	" " "	
" "	No.9. L.A.C. Battery.	200	" " "	
28-4-17	7th Dragoon Guards.	9,000.	S.A.A.	
30-4-17	5th Lancers	3,200.	" " "	
" "	20th Deccan Horse.	2,000.	" " "	

[Signature]
Lieut. a.e.c
o.c. 5th Cavalry Divisional
Ammunition Park.

CONFIDENTIAL

WAR DIARY

of

1st Cavalry Div. Am: PARK

May 1st to 31st 1917

Vol.29.

From 1st May to 30th June 1917

Serial No: 55.

WAR DIARY or INTELLIGENCE SUMMARY.

Army Form C. 2118.

Sheet 1.

Hour, Date, Place	Summary of Events and Information	Remarks and references to Appendices
TINCOURT. MAY 1st	10 lorries on Divisional fatigues - Weather fine.	
2nd	S.A.A. drawn from Railhead for No. 9 L.A.C. Bty. & Amm. Col. - 10 lorries on Divisional fatigues -	
3rd	S.A.A. issued to 5th Cav. Div. Amm. Col. - 8 lorries each day to CAIX, up to May 9th to convey French huts to forward Divisional Area. 2 lorries detached at R.E. Field Sqdn. for fatigues up to May 9th -	
4th	Standing Detail.	
5th	S.A.A. drawn from R.H.A. & held on charge for Amm. Col.	
6th, 7th, 8th & 9th	Lorries on Standing Details CAIX & R.E. F.S. Sqdn.	
10th	21 lorries conveying Amm. from TINCOURT Railhead to R.C.H.A. Brigade Dump.	
11th & 12th	16 lorries conveying huts each day from CAIX to forward Div. Area under 2/Lt. Chatterton - 2 lorries detached 5th F.S. Sqdn. R.E.	
13th	8 lorries on duty at CAIX under 2/Lt. Chatterton. The Park moves from ETALON to POTTE -	
14th	Patrol Webley guns issued to R.C.H.A. Bde. Main Amm. Col. 8 lorries to CAIX under 2/Lt. Chatterton, 1 lorry conveying wheels to Tyre Press at PERONNE - Very heavy storm during night -	

WAR DIARY or INTELLIGENCE SUMMARY.

(Erase heading not required.)

Sheet II

Army Form C. 2118.

Hour, Date, Place	Summary of Events and Information	Remarks and references to Appendices
TINCOURT. MAY 15th	8 lorries on Standing detail at CAIX.	
16th	3 lorries detached, all Field Sqd. R.E's for 3 days (May 18th)	
17th	Pistols Webley Amm' issued to 5th Cav. Div. Amm. Col.	
18th	Nothing to report.	
19th	10 lorries conveying Amm" from TINCOURT Railhead to Corps Dumps at HANCOURT, 5 lorries det. R.E. H. Sql.	
20th	S.A.A & P.W. Amm' to Amm" Col. 3 lorries detached R.E H Sql. 1 lorry taking gun wheels to Amm'n Col.	
21st	The Park moved from POTTE to TINCOURT, & came under O.C. Cavalry Corps Amm" Parks for duty. 3 lorries detached R.E Field Sqs. —	
22nd	3 lorries on Stone fatigues for Cavalry Corps. 9 lorries conveying Amm" from TINCOURT Railhead to Dump at HANCOURT. 3 lorries H. Sqs. R.E's	
23rd	12 lorries on Stone fatigues for Cavalry Corps. 3 lorries detached R.E H. Sql. 1st Cav. Div.	
24th	All "N & NK" Amm" in Park issued to HANCOURT & VILLERS-FAUCON Dumps. 14 lorries on duty conveying Amm" to Corps Dumps. —	

WAR DIARY or INTELLIGENCE SUMMARY

Army Form C. 2118

Sheet III

Place	Date	Hour	Summary of Events and Information	Remarks and references to Appendices
TINCOURT	May 25th		4 lorries on Stone fatigues for Corps. 11 lorries conveying Amm. from Rly Hd. to Dumps.	
	26th		3 pr. Amm. issued to No. 9 L.A.C. Bty. 19 lorries on Stone fatigues for Corps. 1 lorry conveying Tyres to Tyre Press.	
	27th		S.A.A. & No5 Grenades issued to 3rd Cav. Div. Dump. 10 lorries on R.E. fatigues. 5th Cav. Div. Field Sqn.	
	28th		10 lorries on stone fatigues for Corps. 3 lorries moving 59th Div. Artillery to back area.	
	29th		S.A.A. issued to 3rd Cav. Div. Dump & to A.R. Park. Pistol Webley issued to A.R. Park. 16 lorries conveying Amm. from Rly Hd. to Cav. Corps Dumps. 1 lorry on daily fatigues to R.E's. 2 lorries returning unserviceable Amm.	
	30th		S.A.A. 3 pr. Pistol Webley & Grenades No5 taken on charge from 3rd Cav. Div. Amm. Park. S.A.A. & Grenades No5 issued Right Cav. Reserve Bde. 15 lorries conveying R.E. Stores for Cav. Corps.	
	31st		15 lorries conveying R.E. stores for Cav. Corps. 2 lorries on fatigues for 59th Div. 1 lorry to R.E's.	

J. Denny Lieut. A.S.C.
for O/c 5th Cav. D.A.P.

5th Cavalry Divisional Ammunition Park.

Appendix "A" to War Diary
for the month of May=1917.

Date	To whom issued	Nature of Ammn	Number of Rounds	Remarks
2-5-17	No. 9 L.A.C. Battery	S.A.A. 303"	20,000.	
" "	Ammn Col: 5th Cav: Div:	" "	16,000.	
3-5-17	do do	-	16,000.	
14-5-17	Ammn Col: T.C.H.A. Bde.	Pistol bullets	3,064.	
17-5-17	Ammn Col: 5th Cav: Div:	Pistol bullets	1,104.	
20-5-17	Ammn Col: 5th Cav: Div:	S.A.A. 303"	11,000.	
" "	" "	Pistol bullets	828.	
24-5-17	HANCOURT DUMP.	Shrapnel.	1,128.	
" "	" "	H.E.	372.	
" "	VILLERS FAUCON. DUMP.	Shrapnel.	1,125.	
" "	" "	H.E.	372.	
26-5-17	No 9 L.A.C. Battery	3 Pdr.	32.	
27-5-17	3rd Cav: Div: Dumps	S.A.A. 303"	91,000.	
" "	" "	Grenades No 5.	540.	
29-5-17	" "	S.A.A. 303"	40,000.	
" "	A.R.P.	S.A.A. 303"	140,000.	
" "	A.R.P. N 30.a.	Pistol bullets	3960.	
30-5-17	Regtl A.R.P.	S.A.A. 303"	610,000.	
" "	" "	Grenades No 5	1,200.	

Lieut. R.C.C.
G.O.C. 5th C.D.A.P.

Confidential

War Diary
of
5th Cavalry Divn. Amn Pk.

June 1st to 30th 1917

Vol XXX

WAR DIARY
or
INTELLIGENCE SUMMARY.

(Erase heading not required.)

Army Form C. 2118.

Sheet 1

Place	Date	Hour	Summary of Events and Information	Remarks and references to Appendices
TINCOURT	1917 June 1st		S.A.A. issued to 22nd Sqd. R.F.C. Grenades No 5 issued to Cav Corps Park. 19 lorries on duty - fatigues for 59th Div + Cav Corps R.E.'s. Q.M.G. Engineer Cav Corps inspected the Park at 4.30 p.m.	
	2nd		18 lorries on duty on Stone fatigues, + conveying Amm. for Cav Corps. Standing detail of one lorry per day for R.E. fatigues at BUIRE till end of month.	
	3rd		Balance of S.A.A. + Grenades No 5 in Park, handed over to 2nd Cav Div Amm Pk. 19 lorries on duty, Stone + R.E. fatigues for Cav Corps.	
	4th		8 lorries ROISEL Stone fatigues, 4 lorries HANCOURT, conveying Amm.	
	5th		18 lorries on duty Stone + R.E. fatigues for Cavalry Corps. The Inspector of M.T. inspected the lorries in the unit at 5.30 p.m.	
	6th		15 lorries conveying Amm. from BEAUMETZ to Cav Corps Dump.	
	7th		5 lorries Stone fatigues for Corps, 5 lorries at PERONNE for work under R.S.O.	
	8th		7 lorries on duty Corps fatigues.	
	9th		10 lorries on R.E. + Stone fatigues for Cav Corps, 4 lorries conveying Amm. to Dump.	
	10th		13 lorries on R.E. + Stone fatigues for Cav Corps.	
	11th		12 lorries on Stone fatigues for Cav Corps.	

WAR DIARY or INTELLIGENCE SUMMARY

Army Form C. 2118.

Sheet II

Place	Date	Hour	Summary of Events and Information	Remarks and references to Appendices
TINCOURT	1917 June 12th		13 lorries on Stone fatigues for Cav. Corps.	
	13th		16 lorries on Stone fatigues for Cav. Corps. 1 lorry conveying stores for Y.M.C.A. Hut at TINCOURT.	
	14th		8 lorries at MONTIGNY Farm for R.E. fatigues.	
	15th		16 lorries on R.E. & Stone fatigues for Cav. Corps.	
	16th		18 lorries on Stone fatigues for Cav. Corps.	
	17th		15 lorries on Stone fatigues for Cav. Corps.	
	18th		18 lorries conveying Amn. from R.H.d to Cav. Corps Dumps.	
	19th		15 lorries on Stone fatigues for Corps. 2 lorries Amn. duties at LA FLAQUE.	
	20th		13 lorries on Stone fatigues for Corps.	
	21st		8 lorries on fatigues for 5th Cav. Div. R.E.'s. 5 lorries stone fatigues 4 lorries on duty with 4th Cav. Fd. Sqdn. R.E.	
	22nd		18 lorries conveying Amn. from R.H.d to Corps Dumps.	
	23rd		10 lorries on Stone fatigues for Cav. Corps.	
	24th		8 lorries on fatigues for 5th Cav. Div. Fd. Sqd. R.E. 6 lorries stone fatigues for Corps. 1 lorry to Type Press.	

WAR DIARY or INTELLIGENCE SUMMARY

Army Form C. 2118.

Sheet 3.

Place	Date	Hour	Summary of Events and Information	Remarks and references to Appendices
TINCOURT	1917 June 25th		6 lorries on stone fatigues for Corps. 14 lorries conveying shells from R.A.S. to Corps Dumps.	
	26th		16 lorries on stone fatigues for Corps. 3 lorries on duty with Lt. Lt. Col. R.E. 7 lorries moving Amm. Dumps at VERMAND.	
	27th		9 lorries conveying Amm. to Cav Corps Dumps. Lieut A.M. Moloney R.F.A. T. 2/Lieut R.D. Chatterton A.S.C. granted 4 days leave in France.	
	28th		3 lorries on stone fatigues for Corps. 8 lorries moving Amm. Dumps at VERMAND	
	29th		15 lorries on stone fatigues for Cav Corps.	
	30.		6 lorries on stone fatigues & 8 lorries on R.E. Fatigues. Cav Corps.	

J. Denny Lieut. A.S.C.
for O.C. 5th Cav Div. Amm. Pk.

1/7/17

5th Cavalry Divisional Ammn: Park.

Appendix "A" to War Diary

for the month of:- June 1917:-

Date.	To whom issued.	Nature of Ammn:	Number of Rounds.	Remarks.
1-6-17.	22nd Sqd: R.F.C.	S.A.A. .303"	10,000.	
1-6-17.	Cav: Corps Ammn: Park.	Grenades No 5	765.	
3-6-17.	2nd Cav: Ammn: Park.	S.A.A. .303"	236,000.	
		Grenades No 5	420.	
		Gates Wilby	10,145.	

J. Ommy
Lieut: acc.
Comdg: 5th Cav: Divl: Amml: Park

Serial No. 55

5th Cavalry Divisional Ammunition Park.

From 1st to 31st July 1917.

WAR DIARY or INTELLIGENCE SUMMARY.

Army Form C. 2118.

Sheet I

Place	Date	Hour	Summary of Events and Information	Remarks and references to Appendices
TINCOURT	July 1st		18 lorries on Road work for Corps. 1 lorry sent daily to Hospital at BUIRE.	
	2nd		8 lorries conveying Ammn to Dumps. 10 lorries on Road work.	
	3rd		9 lorries on Road work during day. 10 lorries on Road work during night.	
	4th		13 lorries on Road work and 2 conveying trench boards to LE VERGUIER by night. Park inspected at 2.45 pm by G.O.C. 5th Cavalry Divn.	
	5th		12 lorries on Road work for Cav Corps. 2 lorries on R.E. work in LE VERGUIER by night.	
	6th		14 lorries on Road work. 2 lorries on R.E. work.	
	7th		17 lorries on Road work. 2 lorries on R.E. work.	
	8th		5 lorries on Road work. 2 lorries on R.E. work. 5 lorries to ROISEL on R.E. work.	
	9th		3 tn Ammn issued to 3rd Cavalry Ammn Park. 8 lorries on road work. Lt. MOLONEY RFA left the Park to take over command of a section of the 37th Divn Ammn Column.	
	10th		The Park came under the orders of the Divn on the night of the 9th-10th and ceased to be under Cav Corps Ammn Park.	
	11th		1952 rds N and 1048 rds NX drawn from Railhead TINCOURT and the Dump at HANCOURT to refill the Park. 13 tn Ammn now held in proportion of 65% N and 35% NX.	

WAR DIARY
or
INTELLIGENCE SUMMARY.
(Erase heading not required.)

Army Form C. 2118.

Sheet II

Place	Date	Hour	Summary of Events and Information	Remarks and references to Appendices
TINCOURT	July	12th	3 lorries detached for 3 days to convey Cav Corps Signals to AIRE	
		13th	2 lorries detached for duty with Dismounted men of 5th Cav Div for 4 days driving horses	
		14th	2 lorries on duty at Div HQ.	
		16th	Park left TINCOURT at 5.30 am and moved via PERONNE, ALBERT, DOULLENS and FREVENT to ST POL, arriving at 2.30 pm.	
ST POL		22nd	13 lorries out on duty, including 10 helping Supply Column	
		23rd	10 lorries out on Supplies, 3 lorries moving Coal, and 6 lorries for duty with Town Major ST POL. Capt WHITCOMBE returned from attachment at Div HQ and reassumed Command of the Park.	
		24th	5 lorries out on Supplies.	
		25th	6 lorries out on Supplies, 6 lorries on duty with Town Major.	
		26th	5 lorries out on Supplies.	
		27th	1st Section (12 lorries, 1 car, & 2 bicycles) under Lt CHATTERTON left the Park on detachment with RHA Bde and moved via TINQUES and FREVILLERS at 3 pm to GAUCHIN-LEGAL, arriving at 5.30 pm. 1800 Grenades No 5 drawn from Third Army Train to complete Establishment. 3 lorries out on Supplies.	

WAR DIARY or INTELLIGENCE SUMMARY.

Sheet III

Place	Date	Hour	Summary of Events and Information	Remarks and references to Appendices
ST POL	July 28th		13th Section moved from GAUCHIN-LEGAL at 1.30 pm to AIX-NOULETTE.	
	29th		13th Section moved to HERSIN at 3.30 pm and came under the Canadian Corps A.Pk.	

P.S. Whitcombe Capt ASC
Cmdg 5th Can Divn Ammn Park

1/8/17

5th Cavalry Divisional Ammn: Park.

Appendix "H" to War Diary
for the month of July 1914.

Date.	To whom issued	Nature of Ammn: Rounds.	Number of Rounds.	Remarks.
9-7-19	3th Cavalry Ammn; Park.	3 Pdr.	200.	—
27.7.19	19th R.H.A Bde: Ammn: Col:	Shrapnel	3.	
27.7.19	do — do —	H.E.	2.	

J.S. Hirsch Captain. No
OC. 5th C.D.A.P.

CONFIDENTIAL

WAR-DIARY.
of
5th Cavalry Div'n Am'n Park.

August
Vol. XXXII

WAR DIARY
or
INTELLIGENCE SUMMARY.

(Erase heading not required.)

Army Form C. 2118.

Instructions regarding War Diaries and Intelligence Summaries are contained in F. S. Regs., Part II. and the Staff Manual respectively. Title pages will be prepared in manuscript.

Place	Date	Hour	Summary of Events and Information	Remarks and references to Appendices
St. POL	1917 Aug 1st		Ammunition Nil. Rations Lorry on Duty only.	
	2nd		5 Lorries helping Supply Column on Coal fatigues. Capt. P.S. Whitcombe granted 10 days leave to U.K.	
	3rd		Pistols Webley Mark issued to Amm Col. R.H.A. Brigade. Lieut. T. Drury returned from 10 days leave to U.K. & takes command of Park.	
	4th		Nothing to report.	
	5th		5 Lorries on R.E. fatigues during day.	
	6th		Green flares issued to 18th Lancers.	
	7 & 8		Nothing to report.	
	9 & 10		Nothing to report.	
	11th		Nothing to report.	
	12th		Nothing to report.	
	13th		Nothing to report.	
	14th		Capt. P.S. Whitcombe returned from leave to U.K. & resumes command of the Park.	
	15th, 16th, 17th & 18th		Nothing to report.	

WAR DIARY
or
INTELLIGENCE SUMMARY.

(Erase heading not required.)   II.

Army Form C. 2118.

Instructions regarding War Diaries and Intelligence Summaries are contained in F. S. Regs., Part II. and the Staff Manual respectively. Title pages will be prepared in manuscript.

Place	Date	Hour	Summary of Events and Information	Remarks and references to Appendices
St. Pol.	1917 Aug 19th		Lorries on Duty 3. Explosives collected from 2nd Cav. A.P. & issued to units.	
-	20th		3 boxes V.L. 1 inch issued to 8th Hodsons - Gun parts sent up to 13 pr. Sect.	
-	21st		1 lorry with gear box trouble sent down from 13 pr. Section & replaced.	
-	22nd		Capt. P.S. Whitcombe attached to 5th Cav. Div. H.Qs. for Duty. Lieut. J. Drury takes command of Park during his absence.	
-	23rd		Nothing to report	
-	24th		Box of 1 inch pistol issued to Poona Horse.	
-	25th		Nothing to report.	
-	26th		12. Category A men evacuated to Base in accordance with reduced Est. A.D.S.&T. Memo - Cav. Corps P.1255 - 22-8-17	
-	27th 28th 29th		Nothing to report.	
	30 & 31st		2 lorries on Duty.	

13 pr. Section still detached with R.H.A. Brigade.

1/9/17

J. Drury Lieut. A.S.C.
for O/C. 5th Cav. Divn. Amn. Pk.

Appendix "L" to War Diary of :-
5th Cavalry Divisional Ammunition Park.
for the month of August 1914.

Date.	Nature of Ammunition.	Number of Rounds.	Remarks.
To whom issued.			
3-8-14.	14th R.H.A. Bde: Amm: Col. Field bullet	2868.	

J. Army Lewis. a.c.
oc. 5th C.D.A.P.

CONFIDENTIAL

WAR DIARY
of
5th Cavalry Division Ammn Park

SEPTEMBER 1917

Vol XXXIII

# WAR DIARY or INTELLIGENCE SUMMARY.

Army Form C. 2118.

Place	Date	Hour	Summary of Events and Information	Remarks and references to Appendices
ST POL	SEPTEMBER 2nd		Captain P.S. WHITCOMBE returned from duty at Divl Hd Qrs & resumed Command of the Park. Lt J. DRURY relieved 2Lt R.D CHATTERTON in charge of the 18 pr Section detached with Canadian Corps at HERSIN	
	5th		4 Lorries detached for work with Tank Corps at ERIN for 10 days	
	9th		18 pr Section under Lt DRURY returned to Park from attachment to Canadian Corps at HERSIN with 2530 rds "N".	
	13th		Lordsley Car No 1884 transferred to 5th Cavalry Divl Supply Column (Authority O.C.ASC.)	
	14th		2 Motor Cyclists transferred to 5th Cav Supply Col in reduction of Establishment	
	15th		Spare Gun Parts issued to Amn Column at LA THIEULOYE	
	17th		The 4 Lorries detached with Tank Corps returned to the Park	
	18th		8106 rds Pistol Webley drawn from XB BATAUNE and 319,000 rds PAA drawn from ORP DAINVILLE	
	19th		8106 rds Pistol Webley and 319,000 rds PAA issued to Ammn Column at LA THIEULOYE	
	25th		488 rds NX drawn from OPA LIGNY ST FLOCHEL and 1 Smoke ammunition returned	
	26th		198 rds NX issued to Ammn Column and 198 rds NX returned from item and taken on charge	

WAR DIARY
or
INTELLIGENCE SUMMARY.
(Erase heading not required.)

Sheet II

Army Form C. 2118

Hour, Date, Place	Summary of Events and Information	Remarks and references to Appendices
ST POL. September 27th	4 lorries out on Ordnance duties.	
28th	8 lorries out on Ordnance duties.	

P.S. Hitchcock Capt ASC
Comdg 5th Cavalry Ammn Park

1/10/17

Appendix "A" to War Diary of :-
3rd Cavalry Divisional Ammunition Park
for the month of September 1917.

Date.	To whom issued.	Nature of Ammunition	Number of Rounds	Remarks.
19-10-17	17th R.H.A. Bde: Ammunition Col.	S.A.A.	329,000.	
" "	" " " " "	Pistol, Webley	2016.	
26-10-17	" " " " "	H.E.	195.	
27-10-17	" " " " "	H.E.	1.	

P.S. Hiscock
Captain, a/c.
3rd Cav: Div: Amt: Park

CONFIDENTIAL

WAR DIARY
A.
1st Cavalry Division Ammⁿ Park

October 1917

Vol XXXIV

WAR DIARY
or
INTELLIGENCE SUMMARY.
(Erase heading not required.)

Sheet I

Army Form C. 2118

Hour, Date, Place	Summary of Events and Information	Remarks and references to Appendices
ST POL. October 2nd	4 lorries out on Ordnance work.	
3rd	3 lorries out on Ordnance work.	
4th	150,000 rds SAA and 4320 rds Pistol Webley drawn from OPA. (LIGNY)	
5th	300 empty 18pr boxes drawn from OPA (LIGNY) and issued to Am" Column. 1472 rds "N" and 292 rds "NX" collected from Am" Column and handed in at OPA. 18 lorries out on duty. Orders received that Park would probably move North on 8th inst. SAA re-issued to Am" Col. (Appendix "A")	
6th	4 lorries sent to Canadian RDZ and 4 lorries to Seabed RDZ for 2 days for carrying 2nd blankets to new area. 6 lorries out for Ordnance.	
7th	4 lorries sent to Ambala Park for carrying blankets. 9 lorries out for Ordnance and clearing Dump Area. Of the 8 lorries that proceeded with Park on the 6th, 5 returned to Park at ST POL arriving about 10 pm and the remaining 3 were detailed to start drawing ammunition for the AHT Company from "XC" PACIFIC siding just E of POPERINGHE. Park ordered to move to WINNIZEELE tomorrow, 8th inst.	
8th	Park left ST POL at 9.10 am and moved via LILLERS - ST VENANT - HAZEBROUCK - STEENVORDE to WINNIZEELE arriving at 3.30 pm and parked on the STEENVORDE road.	

WAR DIARY
or
INTELLIGENCE SUMMARY.
(Erase heading not required.)

Army Form C. 2118

Sheet II

Hour, Date, Place	Summary of Events and Information	Remarks and references to Appendices
WINNIZEELE October 8th	The 3 lorries at POPERINGHE continued to draw Ammunition for AHT Coy and dumped it near their lines about 1 mile NE of HILLEHOEK. The 4 lorries marching with Ambala Bde arrived at POPERINGHE about 11.30 a.m. and proceeded to "XC" railhead to assist drawing the Am'n. This was completed by 3 p.m. with the help of 12 lorries from the Supply Column. Amm'n drawn:— 1748 rds "N", 952 "NX", and 560,000 rds SAA for AHT Coy and dumped near their lines. 592,000 rds SAA, 2184 rds Pistol Webley, 228 Flares Green and 192 Grenades No 5, to complete Park and Amm'n Column to Establishment.	
9th	Green Flares issued to Regts of Cav and Sirhind Bde.	
10th	2560 Flares Green drawn from "XC" railhead and issued to AHT Coy.	(Appendix "A")
11th	Proportion of Spare Gun parts issued to AHT Coy.	
12th	SAA & Gun parts issued to Amm'n Column near WATOU.	(Appendix "A")
13th	All 13 pr Am'n in Park inspected by I.O.O., and 1038 rds "N" and 16 "NX" condemned owing to damp fuzes. 4 lorries sent to Ambala Bde to carry 2nd Blankets during move of Brigade.	

WAR DIARY
or
INTELLIGENCE SUMMARY.

(Erase heading not required.)

Army Form C. 2118

Sheet III

Hour, Date, Place	Summary of Events and Information	Remarks and references to Appendices
WINNIZEELE October. 14th	2464 rds "N" and 242 "NX" (of which 1038 "N" and 16 "NX" defective) 540,000 rds SAA and 2560 tins flares green returned to XC railhead. 17 lorries returning Amm" to Railhead, 4 detached with Ambala Bde and 4 left at 4 pm to march with Secbad Bde. Orders rec'd that Park would move South on 17th inst.	
15th	4 lorries left at 4 pm to march with Cav. Bde. 8 lorries detached moving blankets for Secbad & Ambala Bdes and 10 lorries helping Supply Column with Supplies.	
16th	12 lorries carrying blankets for Divs and 10 helping Supply Col.	
17th	1748 rds "N", 952 "NX" and 540,000 rds SAA taken over from Amm. Col. at L.16.C.33, S.W. of POPERINGHE. 8 lorries from Ambala & Secbad Bdes rejoined Park at 5.30 pm. Park ordered to move to FRUGES tomorrow 18th inst. 4 lorries returned from Supply Column to escort move and the 4 lorries with Cav. Bde ordered to rejoin at FRUGES.	
18th	Park left WINNIZEELE at 9 am and moved via STEENVOORDE HAZEBROUCK - AIRE - THEROUANNE - to FRUGES, arriving at 3 pm and parked in the Square. 4 lorries from Cav. Bde rejoined at 5 pm and the 4 lorries from Supply Col were returned at 3.30 pm.	

WAR DIARY or INTELLIGENCE SUMMARY.

Army Form C. 2118.

Sheet IV.

Hour, Date, Place	Summary of Events and Information	Remarks and References to Appendices
FRUGES October 19	All Ammⁿ dumped. 19 lorries out, (10 on Supplies work and 5 to BOULOGNE with party for Remounts.)	
" 20	19 lorries out, (10 on Supplies and 5 at BOULOGNE)	
" 21	Defective Ammⁿ exchanged with "N" Battery RHA. 13 lorries on duty. 3 from BOULOGNE returned at 3 pm.	Appendix "A"
" 22^d) 23^d)	Half the lorries in the Park out on various fatigues.	
" 24	Defective Ammⁿ exchanged with Ammⁿ Column at VERCHOQ	Appendix "A"
" 25	1167 rds N and 264 NX defective handed in at Ammⁿ Repair Depot BOULOGNE and new drawn from DANNES to replace. 17 lorries out. (5 Ammⁿ and 8 drawing Signal stores).	
" 26	180 rds "N" of the Ammⁿ drawn from "XC" railhead found defective, round to damp fuzes & report sent in to Divⁿ. 16 lorries out (10 on Supplies).	
" 29	Defective Ammⁿ exchanged with Ammⁿ Column at VERCHOQ	Appendix "A"
" 30	12 pr Ammⁿ issued to 3rd Cavalry MT Coy. 15 lorries out on various duties.	Appendix "A"
" 31st	SAA issued to Cav Bde HQ. 10 lorries out. Total lorry mileage for month -	Appendix "A"

P.S. Hitchcock Capt ASC
Com^d 5th Cavalry Divⁿ Ammⁿ Park.

1/11/17

Appendix "B" to War Diary of :-
5th Cavalry Divisional Ammunition Park.
for the month of October 1917.

Date.	Nature of Amm'n: issued.	Nature of Ammunition.	Number of Rounds.	Remarks.
5-10-17	17th R.H.A. Bde: Amm'n: Col:	S.A.A. "303"	137,000	
" "	"	Pistol Webley	4,320	
10.10.17	A.H.T. Coy; 5th Cav: Div:	Lewis Flares	2560	
12.10.17	17th R.H.A. Bde: Amm'n: Col:	S.A.A. "303"	9,000	
12.10.17	"	Grenades no 5	192	
"	"	Pistol Webley	456	
12.10.17	Ambulance Bde: 5th Cav: Div:	Lewis Flares	1,000	
20.10.17	N. Battery R.H.A. 5th Cav: Div:	Shrapnel 18 pdr.	123 ×	× in exchange
		H.E.	6 ×	for defective.
24.10.17	17th R.H.A. Bde: Amm'n: Col:	Shrapnel	1084 ×	× in exchange
		H.E.	258 ×	for defective
29.10.17	17th R.H.A. Bde: Amm'n: Col:	Shrapnel	170 ×	× in exchange
		H.E.	4 ×	for defective
30.10.17	3rd Cav: Div: M.T. Coy.	Shrapnel	900	
31.10.17	Cav: Cav: Bde: N.C.Os.	S.A.A. "303"	2,000	

S. Whitechie Captain, ASC
Comdg. 5th Cav: Div: Amm'n: Park

CONFIDENTIAL

War Diary

of

1st Cavalry Division Amn Park

From Nov 1st – 16th Inclusive

Vol XXXV

WAR DIARY or INTELLIGENCE SUMMARY.

(Erase heading not required.)

Army Form C. 2118.

Sheet I

Place	Date	Hour	Summary of Events and Information	Remarks and references to Appendices
FRUGES	November 1st, 2nd, 3rd		Half the Lorries of the Park out on various duties, principally Ordnance.	
	4th		13p Ammn which had been reported defective inspected by I.O.O. and 350 rds "N" and 4 rds "NX" Condemned. 13 Lorries out on duty.	
	5th, 6th, 7th		Half the Lorries out on duty for Signals, Ordnance etc.	
	8th		25% of the Explosives in charge of units collected for Exchange. 350 rds "N" and 4 "NX" Exchanged for new at No 19 Ordnance Depot DANNES. 4 Lorries sent to Amiens Park and 4 to Corps Park for carriage of 2nd Hussars on the march South. 23 Lorries out on duty altogether.	
	9th		Explosives collected from Regts Exchanged for new at BOULOGNE. 4 Lorries sent to Sec'ond Park for carriage of 2nd Hussars on move South. 10 Lorries left at 1 pm under Lt DRURY to FINS, stopping the night at DOULLENS En Route, for transport of Supplies and drawing Ammn.	
	10th		All Lorries not working with the Divn. The Lorry detached at CAYEUX returned to Park about 9 am. Orders received for Skeleton Headquarters of Park, comprising CO, 1 Subaltern, 1 MSM, 1 CSM, 1 CQMS and 2 Sgts to proceed to refit at LA BARAQUE CALAIS.	

WAR DIARY or INTELLIGENCE SUMMARY

Army Form C. 2118.

Sheet II

Hour, Date, Place	Summary of Events and Information	Remarks and References to Appendices
FRUGES. November 11th	All lorries out with Division. In accordance with Orders rec'd L/Chatterton, MSM Spalding, and CSM Peroddy left the Park for CALAIS.	
12th, 13th	All lorries out with Div'n.	
14th	Lorries from Div'n returned to Park about 1 pm. Orders rec'd for Park to move to LA CHAPELETTE tomorrow.	
15th	Park left FRUGES at 7 am and moved via ST POL – DOULLENS – ALBERT, and BRAY to LA CHAPELETTE, arriving at 5 pm.	
16th	10 lorries out on RE work. Great flares collected from Amm Coy & together with those from Park returned to Railhead at QUIVCONCE. Red flares taken over from Amm Coy to replace. Under instructions from the Div'n, the whole of the vehicles, personnel, and ammunition of the Park, with the following exceptions*, were handed over to the OC, 5th Cavalry Supply Column, and form a section of the Supply Column from today. * The CO, Capt. P.S. Whitcombe ASC to Div'l HdQrs, the COMS and 2 Sgts to LA BARAQUE CALAIS	P.P. Whitcombe Capt. ASC Comd'g 5th Cavalry Div'n Am Park 16/11/17

(9 20 6) W 3332—1107 100,000 10/13 H W V Forms/C. 2118/10.

5th Cavalry Divisional Ammn Park.

Appendix B to War Diary for period —
1st November 17 to 30th November 1917.

Date	To whom issued	Nature of ammunition.	Number of Rounds.
5th Nov.	1st Dragoon Guards	S.A.A.	6000.
"	20th Decean Horse	"	8000.
"	13th Machine Gun Squadron	"	10,000.
5th Nov.	N-19 Advanced Depot	N.K.	350. } *
	* Defective	N.K.	4. } *

* Defective.

G.P.Mitchell Capt. a/cc
Comdg. 5th Cavalry Divl.
A. Park.

www.ingramcontent.com/pod-product-compliance
Lightning Source LLC
Chambersburg PA
CBHW081238170426
43191CB00034B/1967